From Slave to
Civil War Hero

Also by Michael L. Cooper

PLAYING AMERICA'S GAME:
The Story of Negro League Baseball

From Slave to Civil War Hero
The Life and Times of Robert Smalls

by Michael L. Cooper

A RAINBOW BIOGRAPHY

LODESTAR BOOKS
Dutton   New York

to my brother, Ron

Library of Congress Cataloging-in-Publication Data

Cooper, Michael L.
From slave to Civil War hero: the life and times of Robert Smalls/ by Michael L. Cooper.—1st ed.
p. cm.—(A Rainbow biography)
Includes bibliographical references and index.
ISBN 0-525-67489-6
1. Smalls, Robert, 1839–1915—Juvenile literature.   2. Afro-Americans—Biography—Juvenile literature.   3. United States—History—Civil War, 1861–1865—Participation, Afro-American—Juvenile literature.   4. Legislators—South Carolina—Biography—Juvenile literature.   5. Afro-American legislators—South Carolina—Biography—Juvenile literature.   6. Reconstruction—South Carolina—Juvenile literature.   [1. Smalls, Robert, 1839–1915 2. Afro-Americans—Biography 3. Legislators.   4. United States—History—Civil War, 1861–1865—Participation, Afro-American. 5. Reconstruction—South Carolina.]
I. Title.   II. Series.
E185.97.S6C66   1994
973.8'092—dc20
[B]   93-44169
                                                                    CIP
                                                                     AC

Published in the United States by Lodestar Books, an affiliate of Dutton Children's Books, a division of Penguin Books USA Inc., 375 Hudson Street, New York, New York 10014

Published simultaneously in Canada by McClelland & Stewart, Toronto

Editor: Virginia Buckley
Designer: Richard Granald, LMD

Printed in the U.S.A. First Edition
10 9 8 7 6 5 4 3 2 1

Contents

From Slave to Hero   1

1   Escape from Slavery   4

2   Childhood in Bondage   12

3   Black Hero   20

4   Fighting the Rebels   29

5   Incident in Philadelphia   36

6   War's End   39

7   King of Beaufort   47

8   The End of an Era   55

Glossary   61

Chronology   65

Index   69

Robert Smalls, the slave who became a hero

From Slave to Hero

One of the most daring and heroic adventures since the war commenced was undertaken and successfully accomplished by a party of Negroes in Charleston on Monday night last. Nine colored men, comprising the pilot . . . and the crew of the rebel gun-boat *Planter,* took the vessel under their exclusive control, passed the batteries and forts in Charleston harbor, hoisted a white flag, [and] ran out to the blockading squadron."

Harper's Weekly, May 1862

The young man piloting the *Planter* was Robert Smalls, the first slave to become a widely known Civil War hero. Smalls's fame and intelligence enabled him to become an important black leader in the difficult years after the war. Although he was one of the most prominent African-Americans of his time, a great deal about him is not known.

His life was obscured by slavery and racism. Educating slaves was against the law, so Smalls did not learn to read or write until he was an adult and free. He never recorded his memories of his life as a slave or his thoughts as a political leader. What we know about Smalls is pieced together from interviews, letters, official documents, and newspaper accounts.

Even though incomplete, these sources provide a fascinating view of a man who was both exceptional and ordinary. He was exceptional because he rose from slavery to political fame by bravely and persistently fighting the very thing that made his life most difficult—racism. He was ordinary because 4 million other ex-slaves were in the same difficult fight.

When the Civil War began in 1861, slavery had existed in the United States for over 250 years. This practice of owning black men, women, and children had been gradually abolished in the North. But southern states clung to the system because they depended on the labor of their slaves.

By the 1850s, a growing number of people wanted to end slavery. The argument between anti-slavery people, who were called abolitionists, and pro-slavery people grew so bitter that it led to war.

After Abraham Lincoln was elected president in November 1860, eleven southern states seceded from the United States. They seceded because they thought Lincoln opposed slavery. These states created a new country called the Confederate States of America. The North, which was still called the United States, or the Union, did not want the South to secede. Tension between the two regions grew to a climax in Charleston, South Carolina, on April 12, 1861. That day Confederate cannons fired on the U.S. fort in Charleston harbor, Fort Sumter, and started the Civil War.

Seven months after war began, a fleet of Union ships captured Port Royal Sound, only fifty miles south of Charleston. This victory gave the United States navy control of a good harbor, the town of Beaufort, and several large islands, which are known as the Sea Islands. With Port Royal as a base, Union ships were able to blockade the major port cities of Savannah, Georgia, and Charleston. They kept confederate ships from delivering valuable cotton to England and prevented Charleston from receiving badly needed supplies.

This story about a man who escaped from slavery and fought for freedom and equality for millions of fellow African-Americans begins soon after the capture of Port Royal.

1

Escape from Slavery

Blockade duty for the *U.S.S. Onward* was uneventful most days, but not May 13, 1862.

It was just after 5 A.M. Night was fading to soft morning light. Thick patches of gray fog hung over the Atlantic Ocean. The sailor on watch suddenly started. Through the fog he saw something big and dark coming directly at his ship. A boat! But what kind? An enemy blockade runner? Or a warship making a surprise attack?

Clang! Clang! Clang! The watchman's bell sounded the alarm. At that early hour the *Onward*'s crew was fast asleep. When the sailors heard the urgent clanging, they jumped from their bunks and rushed to their battle stations. Load the cannons, the captain shouted, prepare to fire! Just in time, the rebel ship raised a white flag, the traditional sign of surrender.

The captain ordered the mysterious vessel to pull alongside. Armed with rifles and pistols, several sailors boarded the ship. They found a group of scared-looking black people—nine men, five women, and three young children. Suspecting hidden enemy troops, the sailors cautiously searched the boat. They did not find any Confederate soldiers aboard, only four cannons and two hundred rounds of ammunition.

One of the blacks, a short, husky young man, stepped forward. He identified himself as Robert. Everyone on the ship was a slave, he explained. They had risked their lives to steal this cotton steamer, named the *Planter*, out of heavily guarded Charleston harbor.

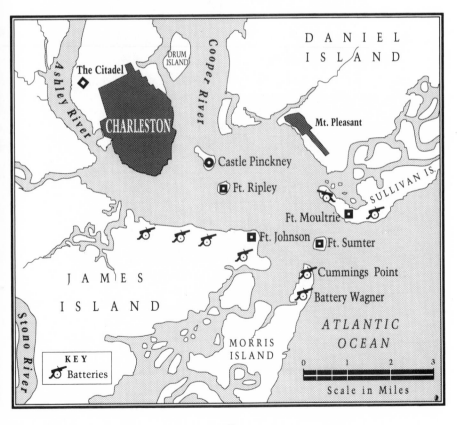

Robert Smalls and three other sailors
who escaped with the Planter

The *Planter*, Robert related, had been ferrying lumber, brick, slave laborers, cannons, and ammunition to the many new fortifications being built around Charleston. Four forts and dozens of batteries, which are clusters of cannons, protected the important South Carolina city from attack by Union forces.

Three white men—a captain, an engineer, and a first mate—had been in charge of the *Planter*. The rest of the crew were slaves. Robert was the pilot, the man who steered the vessel. He was expert at avoiding the harbor's dangerous currents and sand bars that might wreck the boat. Soon after northern forces had invaded South Carolina, capturing the small town of Beaufort and several large islands south of Charleston, Robert and his black shipmates planned their escape. For over six months they anxiously waited for the right moment. Their chance came when they learned that the white crewmen were planning to go ashore overnight.

On the morning of May 13, several hours before sunrise, the nervous black sailors lit a fire in the ship's steam boiler. They were startled when the ocean breeze carried the fire's thick smoke across the wharf and down city streets. They prayed that the smoke would not draw a sentry's attention. Quickly the crew released the moorings, and the *Planter* slid away from the wharf.

Before steaming the four miles through the

harbor to open ocean, the ship stopped briefly to take aboard the wives and children of the crew. These new fugitives included Robert's wife, Hannah, and their infant son and four-year-old daughter. Then the crew turned the *Planter* east toward the Atlantic Ocean and the Union navy.

It was a dangerous journey. Not only were the people aboard the *Planter* runaway slaves, they also were stealing the best boat in Charleston. And it was loaded with valuable cannons and ammunition scheduled for delivery to a Confederate fort that very day. If captured, the black men aboard the *Planter* would be immediately hanged.

Robert guided the steamer expertly through the dark harbor. He wore the white captain's straw hat, and from afar no one could possibly see whether the pilot was white or black. The ship steamed directly toward Charleston's main fort, Sumter, which guarded the harbor entrance.

Before passing the five-story brick fort, the *Planter* had to give the proper signal on its whistle. Robert hoped the sentry would not question why this boat was going out at such an early hour. As the ship neared the fort, Robert gave the signal—two long blasts and one short blast—on the steam whistle. No challenge came from Sumter's guard. The *Planter* steamed safely toward open sea.

"The sentinel on the parapet called for the corporal of the guard and reported the guard boat going out," Sumter's commanding officer later explained.

The Planter *was used first by the
Confederates and then by the Union to
transport troops and supplies.*

U.S. NAVAL HISTORICAL CENTER

"It is by no means unusual for the guard boat to run out at that hour, and no further notice was taken of that occurrence."

The Confederates were furious. A Charleston newspaper called the escape "extraordinary . . . our community was intensely agitated Tuesday morning by the intelligence that the steamer *Planter* had been taken possession of by her colored crew, steamed up and boldly ran out to the blockaders."

A Confederate newspaper in Richmond, Virginia, complained that it was "one of the most shameful events in this or any other war . . . an incident that should consign the military authorities of that city . . . to petticoats or strait jackets for the rest of the war."

The Confederate commanders in Charleston were embarrassed and angry. They punished the white crewmen who had been in charge of the ship by sending them to prison. And they posted a bounty for Robert. A Union newspaper mocked the Southerners: "It is stated that the authorities of Charleston have offered a reward of four thousand dollars for Small. He does not, however, propose to return to the rebels until his services can be made available in conducting a Union fleet into the harbor of the cradle of the rebellion."

When Admiral Samuel DuPont, the commander in charge of the U.S. blockade of Charleston, heard about the *Planter*, he sent for the ship's pilot. After hearing the story, DuPont said the escape was "one of the coolest and most gallant naval acts of war." Then the admiral described Robert as a man "superior to any who have come into our lines, intelligent as many have been."

Admiral DuPont surprised people by calling Robert intelligent and superior. Most white people thought slaves, all blacks in fact, were dumb and inferior. But Robert, even when a slave, proved them wrong.

2

Childhood in Bondage

Robert was born at home in the little town of
Beaufort on April 5, 1839. His home, next to a
kitchen, was a small room called the slave quarters. Both the kitchen and the quarters stood
behind a simple, two-story house owned by the
McKee family.

This white family also owned Robert and his
mother, Lydia. Slaves did not have last names, so
mother and child were known only by their first
names. Ever since she had been a young girl, Lydia
had worked in the McKee home. She cooked,
cleaned, and waited on Mr. McKee, his wife, and
their five children.

Nothing is known about Robert's father. Some
people thought he was a white man because of
Robert's light skin. Even if he was a slave, Robert's
father would not have been married to the boy's
mother. Slaves were not allowed to marry. Some
had marriage ceremonies, but these were not legal
marriages, and their family life was very different
from the lives of white families. Slave children
belonged to the mother's owner. He could beat
them, rent them to a neighbor, or even sell them.

Their parents might protest, but the owner had the final word.

Unlike Robert and his mother, most slaves lived on cotton or rice plantations. These two crops were so widely grown along the South Carolina coast that they were called King Cotton and Queen Rice. The McKees owned dozens of slaves who worked on the family's cotton plantation on Ladies Island, which was across the bay from Beaufort.

When Robert was a child, over ten thousand slaves lived on the Sea Islands near Beaufort. Some of these people remembered their original homes

Former slaves in the fields on Edisto Island near Beaufort. This photograph was taken only a few weeks after the Union navy and army captured Port Royal Sound.

in faraway Africa. All of them were the children and grandchildren of Africans. Sea Island slaves, like Robert, spoke a language of their own called Gullah, which combined African and English words.

Men, women, and even young children did the planting, the harvesting, and every other job required to run the large plantations. Although slaves lived in small shacks, were poorly fed, and worked constantly, few dared complain.

Those who did complain or neglected their tasks could be whipped. This was a common way to punish slaves. Robert saw many black people cruelly beaten. "My aunt was whipped so many a time until she has not the same skin she was born with," he said.

Robert had an easier life than most plantation slaves because he was a house servant. He ate leftovers from the McKees' meals, wore the McKee boys' old clothing, and learned to speak English as well as white people. Robert might have been the personal servant of Henry, the oldest son in the McKee family.

The young slave would have slept on the floor at the foot of Henry McKee's bed. There he could be awakened in the night to fetch his master a glass of water or the chamber pot. When Henry rode his horse to a neighbor's house or down to the dock, little Robert would run along beside the horse. While his master visited friends or attended to business, Robert tended the horse. This was a privileged childhood for any young slave, but it did not last long.

When Robert was only twelve years old, Henry took him to work in Charleston, some fifty miles up the coast. Robert quickly discovered that slave life in a city was very different from slave life on a plantation or in a small town.

The old colonial city straddled the peninsula between the Ashley and the Cooper rivers. On the tip of this peninsula, overlooking the harbor formed by the two rivers, stood the city's most stately houses. These homes, owned by wealthy rice and cotton planters, had commanding views of broad Charleston harbor. When Robert arrived in Charleston in 1851, about forty thousand people lived there. Half were black; some of these blacks were free but most were slaves.

Bondsmen filled the streets and open-air markets, running errands, shopping, and selling fruits, vegetables, and fish. Visitors to the city often thought blacks far outnumbered whites. As one English traveler noted, the "great numbers of darkies is very striking at first. You see, even in the main streets, two or even three of these to every white man, and in the back streets you see no one else." Most Charleston homes, even those belonging to free blacks, were cared for by one or two slaves. These servants were usually women who cooked meals, washed clothes, cleaned houses, and nursed white babies. Male slaves drove carriages, labored on the wharves, and worked in the hotels.

At first, Robert's master found work for him, and kept all of the money that the boy earned. In one job the young slave tended streetlamps. Every day at dusk the boy walked along Charleston's cobblestone streets lighting the gas lamps. He also was a waiter at the popular Planters Hotel. At the hotel and elsewhere, Robert often heard Southerners defending slavery. Black people, slavery's advocates argued, were not like white people. They were not smart enough to live free, so bondage was good for them.

When he was a teenager, Robert asked Henry McKee's permission to find his own jobs. This practice, called hiring out, was common among city slaves. It gave them more freedom and a chance to find a job they liked. Robert promised to pay his master fifteen dollars every month.

In addition to hiring out, Robert also lived out. This meant he lived away from his master's house. Many city slaves lived out. Some rented rooms or small houses. Others slept where they worked. A visitor to Charleston described returning to his hotel late at night and stumbling over sleeping servants. The hotel's black staff had "already lain down for the night in the passages with their clothes on. They had neither beds nor bedding, and you may kick them or tread upon them with impunity." Despite the hardships, slaves liked living out because they escaped their owners' watchful eyes. Masters permitted it to avoid the expense of housing and feeding their bondsmen.

Living out and hiring out gave slaves a little freedom, but they were never entirely free of bondage. Charleston's city officials controlled the large slave population in various ways. No slaves were allowed to learn to read or write. They had to wear metal identification tags. They could not leave their masters' or employers' homes or businesses without a written pass stating where they were going. And bondsmen were not allowed on the streets after 9 P.M., when the bells of St. Michael's Episcopal Church tolled the curfew.

To enforce these laws, militia patrolled the city day and night. Violators were taken to jail, and Charleston's mayor decided their punishment. An offense like breaking curfew might bring ten lashes with a bullwhip.

Robert seemed determined to free himself of many of slavery's burdens. Since, as a slave, he lacked a last name, he made one up. Robert was a small man. Fully grown, he was only five feet, five inches tall. Because of his size, people referred to him as small Robert. To create a last name, he simply reversed the words so he was known as Robert Small. Several years later he added an *s* to his new name.

In the mid-1850s, Robert "married" a slave woman named Hannah. He married, he once

The earliest known photograph of Robert Smalls. It was probably taken soon after his escape.

Hannah Smalls after the war

explained, for practical reasons. "My idea was to have a wife to prevent me from running around—to have somebody to do for me and to keep me. The colored men in taking wives always do so with reference to the service the women will render." It is not known exactly where Robert and Hannah lived. Perhaps they both slept where they worked. Or maybe they rented a cheap room. They probably had few possessions other than some clothing and cooking utensils.

Robert was clearly an ambitious young man determined to improve his status as much as possible. He went to work on Charleston's docks in the late 1850s. First he was a stevedore, a person who loads and unloads ships. Later he was a sailmaker, and then a sailor. He joined the slave crew of the *Planter* soon after a local ship builder launched the 147-foot cotton steamer in 1860. This sidewheeler could carry fourteen hundred bales of cotton on its three decks and easily navigate the shallow rivers and bays around the Sea Islands.

When the Civil War began in the spring of the following year, the *Planter* and its slave crew were commandeered by the Confederate army. The army was hurriedly building defenses to protect Charleston against invasion by the Union.

Black people were very important to the defense of Charleston and of South Carolina. "The labor of our slaves," wrote one official, "scarce less than the gallantry and endurance of our noble soldiers, has preserved thus far our cherished old city and loved state."

The *Planter* was under the command of Brigadier-General Roswell Ripley. He was the highest ranking Confederate officer in Charleston. The ship was outfitted with two cannons, one fore and one aft, but it was not a gunboat. Rather, it was a transport. The *Planter* transported guns, ammunition, and troops to the new forts defending Charleston.

Robert piloted the *Planter* for the Confederate army for almost a year before his daring escape made him a popular hero.

3

Black Hero

After he stole the *Planter* from Confederate Charleston in the spring of 1862, Robert Smalls was no longer an unknown southern slave; he was a free and famous man.

Smalls was invited to New York City to appear at Shiloh Church, where many prominent black leaders had denounced slavery. "Nearly all of the colored men of New York and Brooklyn," a local newspaper reported, greeted the ex-slave with a "wild and enthusiastic outburst of feeling." The crowd wanted "to do special honor to a recognized hero, who has honored not only himself but his race. . . . The entire audience . . . rose and received him with demonstrations of extreme delight."

They presented the boat pilot a large gold medal with an engraving of the *Planter* on one side. On the reverse side of the medal, an inscription read, "To Robert Small by the colored citizens of New York, Oct. 2, 1862, as a token of their regard for his heroism, his love of liberty, and his patriotism."

The large crowd at Shiloh Church greeted Smalls enthusiastically because he was living proof of the bravery of black men. Not everyone believed that ex-slaves were capable of courage. A Northerner working among the former bondsmen in the Sea Islands expressed a common belief of white people in 1862: "Negroes—plantation Negroes at least—will never make soldiers in one generation. Five white men could put a regiment to flight."

This and other prejudices made President Lincoln reluctant to allow African-Americans to join the Union army. Hoping to change the president's mind, Smalls accompanied Reverend Mansfield French, a white preacher, to Washington, D.C., where the two men met with the Secretary of War, Edwin M. Stanton. Former bondsmen would make good soldiers, argued Reverend French, and he pointed to Smalls as a prime example of the courage of black people.

The final decision on whether to allow blacks to become Union soldiers rested with President Lincoln. After much deliberation, Lincoln finally decided to recruit black soldiers. The Secretary of War gave Smalls a letter to carry back to South Carolina. This letter ordered General Rufus Saxton to recruit "colored persons of African descent . . . and muster them into the service of the United States for the term of the war." All black men who served, and their wives and children, would be "forever free." By war's end, some 175,000 soldiers, nearly one-sixth of the men who joined the Union army, were African-American.

The First South Carolina Volunteers, organized in the Sea Islands in November 1862, was the army's first regiment of ex-slaves. Organizing this regiment, popularly known as the First South, was not easy.

Beaufort had been a sleepy little town when Robert was a slave child in the McKee home. After the Union invasion, it became a bustling military camp occupied by several thousand white soldiers. Ex-slaves, whom Union military officials called contrabands, a word used to describe captured enemy property, also crowded into the town.

Many bondsmen had been left behind when their masters fled the islands. Others had escaped from inland plantations. Thousands of black men and women enslaved in South Carolina and Georgia had slipped through Confederate lines. They hid by day and traveled by night. Some floated in dugout canoes down the Savannah or Coosawhatchie rivers. Or they waded through swamps, risking the danger of being shot by Confederate patrols or of being bitten by deadly water moccasin snakes.

In Beaufort, since they no longer worked on plantations, ex-slaves had little to do and nothing to eat. They often clustered at the old Customs House, where the quartermaster not only gave them army rations but also hired them as cooks and laborers.

Smalls and other influential blacks spoke at churches and schools urging ex-slaves to join the army. When Smalls spoke, he described in exciting detail how he had escaped from slavery on the *Planter*. Then he urged the men to join the army and fight for the freedom of the millions of African-Americans still in bondage.

Some men enlisted voluntarily, but many were afraid. The military reminded them of slavery when white men controlled their lives. These ex-slaves also recalled the warnings of their old masters, who claimed the Yankees would sell them to the dreaded sugarcane plantations in Cuba where the weather was hotter than hell and the slave masters crueler than the devil.

Enlistment was so low that military patrols began taking men from their homes and forcing them to join the army. For many months, black men avoided going to Beaufort, to church, and to other public places where they might be grabbed by Union soldiers. Some hid in the swamps that dotted the islands, relying on families and friends to bring them food. One man, who later proved to be an excellent soldier, was discovered hiding up the chimney of his cabin.

Gradually, ex-bondsmen accepted military service. The black recruits took pride in their uniforms and delighted in the chance to fight their former owners, whom they called "secesh," an abbreviation of the word *secessionist*. But even in the Union army, these men faced a lot of discrimination. White soldiers ridiculed the new recruits.

A poster to recruit black soldiers

The army paid black troops less than white troops. And blacks often waited months before they were given uniforms and guns.

Even famous Robert Smalls did not escape discrimination. One newspaperman reported this exchange when the boat pilot visited Admiral Samuel DuPont, the man in charge of the Union navy in South Carolina. "This boy wants to see the admiral," yelled General Truman Seymour, the admiral's aide, announcing Smalls's arrival. "Will

24

you please let him know that this boy is waiting?" Then, turning to Smalls, he cried out in a sharp voice, "Here boy, you can go aboard, and the officer will tell you when the admiral is ready to see you."

The newspaperman, obviously sympathetic to the black pilot, wrote: "Now Smalls is not a boy; he is a man of, I should think, 30 years and wears a beard sufficient to show it. I blushed for General Seymour when I heard him use the old cant of the slave-master toward this man, who performed one of the bravest and most brilliant acts of the war. General Seymour is himself a brave man and if a white man had done what Smalls did, he would have no doubt honored him for it. But because this gallant fellow happened to have a black skin, he speaks to him in a way that seemed to me . . . contemptibly mean."

Despite the prejudice, eight hundred ex-slaves did join the First South and fought bravely. They guarded Beaufort against Confederate raiders and attacked rebel posts, destroying valuable salt mines in Bluffton, Georgia, and capturing the town of Jacksonville, Florida. News of ex-slaves courageously fighting for the United States silenced northern whites who argued against giving blacks equal rights.

Many other former bondsmen, like Smalls, were employed by the Quartermaster's Department as ship's pilots. This department hired more than a thousand blacks to work on ships, drive wagons, and cook for the Union soldiers and sailors.

No one knows exactly why Smalls did not join the army. One reason, perhaps, is that he received much better pay as a ship's pilot. Black soldiers were promised $13 a month; in 1862 Smalls earned $50 a month, and by the end of the war he was earning $175 a month. Also, his knowledge of the many rivers, inlets, and bays along the coast and, most importantly, of the heavily fortified Charleston harbor, made him more valuable as a pilot than as a soldier.

The courage of Smalls and of the soldiers of the First South changed people's attitudes about ex-slaves. "We did not think a year ago that these people would make soldiers," a Sea Island teacher wrote to friends in the North. "Now it is a matter of fact . . . that they will fight in open warfare."

These changing attitudes made 1862 a very eventful year for Robert Smalls and for all African-Americans. Smalls had freed himself, demonstrating bravery and resourcefulness that impressed many people. And black men had been allowed to join the Union army. Best of all, President Lincoln had decided to strike an important blow against slavery.

Lincoln signed the Emancipation Proclamation, which became law on January 1, 1863. It declared all slaves in ten rebellious states free. Most southern blacks remained in bondage and unaware of

*A black soldier addresses the crowd of freedmen
during the Emancipation Day celebration in the Sea Islands.*
<small>SOUTH CAROLINA HISTORICAL SOCIETY</small>

the proclamation, but Emancipation Day in the Sea Islands was cause for a big celebration.

Early New Year's Day, Smalls was busy ferrying boatload after boatload of ex-slaves to Smith Plantation, where the First South had its camp. The pretty spot was shaded by big oak trees, and there was a nice view of the sparkling Beaufort River. The cloudless blue sky and warm temperature were perfect for a celebration.

Nearly five thousand people gathered beneath the gnarled branches of live oaks draped with gray wisps of Spanish moss. The women wore brightly colored kerchiefs on their heads. The black soldiers, looking splendid in their new uniforms of navy blue jackets and red pants, marched smartly up and down the parade ground while a brass band played lively military music. In preparation for dinner, twelve huge oxen roasted over the dancing flames of hot fires.

For three hours, the crowd sang, prayed, and listened to speeches. A handsome black sergeant named Prince Rivers, who would become an important politician after the war, told the crowd that former bondsmen faced a long, difficult fight before they realized freedom and equality. Another man solemnly read the Emancipation Proclamation. That day, because of the proclamation, former slaves were officially free; henceforth, they were known as freedmen.

Near the end of the ceremony, a freedman expressed his feelings by singing the patriotic song "America." At first the murmuring crowd became silent. Then the voices of thousands of freedmen joined in:

> My country, 'tis of thee,
> Sweet land of liberty,
> Of thee I sing:
> Land where my fathers died,
> Land of the pilgrims' pride,
> From every mountainside
> Let freedom ring.

4

Fighting the Rebels

Although Robert Smalls was not officially in the military, he was in seventeen skirmishes and battles. In one of those battles, the largest naval assault on Charleston, he piloted the lead ship.

On the morning of April 7, 1863, nine strange-looking Union vessels dropped anchor near the entrance to Charleston harbor. Seven of these ships were monitors. They were the *Weehawken, Passaic, Montauk, Patapsco, Catskill, Nantucket,* and *Nahant.* These odd-looking boats were a new kind of steam-powered vessel that resembled modern-day submarines. Their decks were near water level. Each monitor had a tower sticking out of the middle of its deck. This tower held two cannons and a wheelhouse where the pilot steered.

The two remaining vessels, the *Keokuk* and the *New Ironsides,* were ironclads. They were wooden ships covered with iron plates to protect them from cannonballs. The *Keokuk* had two turrets and two cannons. It sat high in the water, a bigger target than the flat monitors. Admiral Samuel DuPont himself commanded the *New Ironsides*. The 3,500-ton ship carried thirty-two guns, sixteen on each side. It was one of the most powerful warships in the world.

While the other eight vessels rested at anchor, Smalls steered the *Keokuk* into the main ship's channel, where he placed buoys to guide the invading navy into the harbor. The rebels had booby-trapped the channel by stringing it with rope webbing to entangle ship propellers and rudders. They had also scattered floating mines, called torpedoes, that exploded on impact with the hull of a ship.

Four forts and dozens of batteries bristling with cannons guarded Charleston harbor. The most menacing fort of all, one Smalls had faced only a year before, was Fort Sumter, protecting the harbor entrance.

By mid-afternoon, Smalls had completed marking the channel with buoys, and the squadron's attack began. The monitors and ironclads steamed single file by fortifications on Morris Island and Sullivan Island. Confederates and Yankees alike waited nervously for the first shot. As the *Weehawken* sailed between Fort Sumter and Fort Moultrie, which was on Sullivan Island less than a mile from Sumter, Moultrie fired first. The cannonball missed the monitor and plunged harmlessly into the water. Then the *Weehawken* fired at Sumter. Its first shot arched over the fort, while a

Charleston harbor before the Civil War. Fort Sumter and Fort Moultrie guard the entrance to the harbor.

second shot struck the thick wall, sending fragments of red brick flying.

Boom! Boom! Boom! Cannons from all around the harbor unleashed a barrage on the little ships, causing confusion in the squadron. DuPont's *New Ironsides* veered off course. It had to drop anchor to avoid running aground. DuPont ordered the other ships to continue the fight. Hundreds of Confederate cannonballs "literally rained around the Union vessels," one observer noted, "splashing the water up thirty feet in the air, and striking and booming from their decks and turrets."

The *Nahant* ventured closest to Sumter and suffered the worst fire. Cannon shot tore through the pilothouse, killing one man and wounding another. The *Keokuk* managed to fire only three shots before shells from Moultrie and Sumter disabled its two cannons. Confederate artillery continued to pound the *Keokuk* for thirty minutes. Ninety-six cannonballs struck the ironclad. Surprisingly, no one on board was killed or even seriously injured. At 5 P.M., after two hours of fighting, DuPont signaled his ships to retreat.

The Union forces had managed to fire only 139 shots, most of those at Sumter. The few shots that struck the big fort did little damage. Four rebels were killed and ten wounded. Many of these casualties were caused by the accidental explosion of a cannon at Battery Wagner. The Confederates fired over 2,200 shots, hitting their targets at least 500 times. One man was killed and twenty-two men were wounded on the *Nahant* and the *Keokuk*. Smalls's battered ironclad limped out of the harbor. The next morning, after another ship had picked up the crew, the *Keokuk* sank.

The Union forces had suffered a humiliating loss, but military leaders in Washington were determined to capture the cradle of the rebellion. Three months after the navy's failed assault, the Fifty-fourth Massachusetts Infantry, the first all-black regiment recruited in the North, led a twilight attack on Battery Wagner. This earthen fort straddled a narrow slip of land on Morris Island. The regiment's white commanding officer, Colonel Robert Gould Shaw, led the charge until he was stopped dead by a bullet through the heart. In the fierce two-hour battle, which included hand-to-hand combat within the fort, more than 250 men from the Fifty-fourth Massachusetts were killed or wounded. Although the attack had failed, the bravery of these black soldiers impressed the nation. "Through the cannon smoke of that dark night," one magazine article declared, "the manhood of the colored race shines before many eyes that would not see."

There were no more major attacks on Charleston after the summer of 1863. Union forces continued their blockade of the South Carolina city, engaging in numerous skirmishes on land and at sea. During one of these brief battles, Smalls again proved himself a hero. The *Planter* was delivering food to Union soldiers camped on an island near Charleston. As the ship steamed up Folly Creek, by the hamlet of Secessionville on James Island, a hidden Confederate battery suddenly opened fire with rifles and small cannons.

Bullets showered the wooden vessel like deadly hail, and the steamer's captain panicked. He ran from the pilothouse and hid in the boiler room below deck. Without a commander, Smalls knew that his ship would be captured. The pilot also knew the Confederates would take the white crew

Robert Smalls on the deck of the Planter. *His uniform is believed to have belonged to the ship's former Confederate captain.*

as prisoners. But the rebels hated ex-slaves and would slaughter the black crewmen. Smalls took charge and steered the *Planter* away from the Confederate guns. He saved the ship and all of its men.

The army report describing the incident praised Smalls and gave him the nonmilitary title of captain of the *Planter.* "He is an excellent pilot, of undoubted bravery, and is in every respect worthy of the position. This is due him as a proper recognition of his heroism and services. The present captain is a coward, though a white man. Dismiss

This drawing of the Planter *accompanied a* Harper's Magazine *article about Smalls.*

him, therefore, and give the steamer to this brave black Saxon."

As 1863 came to an end, Charleston stood unconquered. Union forces had been unable to capture the city. But Robert Smalls still had many battles to fight.

5

Incident in Philadelphia

In the spring of 1864, Captain Smalls sailed the *Planter* eight hundred miles north up the Atlantic coast to the Philadelphia Naval Yard to have new boilers installed. The repairs required months of work. Smalls probably thought he had left the war behind. But he found a different kind of fighting in the old Pennsylvania city.

Philadelphia had one of the largest free black populations in the United States. Over twenty thousand African-Americans lived there. Even though they were free, black people in that big city were treated as second-class citizens. Most were poor. They could work only as domestics and laborers. They were not allowed to vote or attend public schools. Despite their hardships, Philadelphia blacks were eager to help newly freed slaves in the South.

Captain Smalls threw himself into the task of raising money to buy food, clothing, and school-books for freedmen in the Sea Islands. His meetings with church groups and local black leaders made him a well-known figure in Philadelphia's black community. An incident in early winter assured he would be remembered long after he returned to South Carolina.

Several Philadelphia companies operated horse-drawn streetcars. They were a popular way of traveling about the large city, at least for white people. Most streetcars did not allow black riders. And those few that did frequently made their African-American passengers stand outside the car on open platforms. Some blacks who had refused to give up their seats had been beaten by angry whites.

Black leaders complained to the streetcar companies and to city officials about this unfair treatment. They pointed out that hundreds of local black men had joined the Union army and were training in Camp Penn outside the city. The soldiers' families were unable to visit the training camp because they were not allowed to ride the streetcars and had no other transportation.

One cold and rainy day in early winter, Smalls and a sailor friend, a white man, were riding the Thirteenth Street car from the naval yard to downtown Philadelphia. Because of the rain, they sat inside. The car became filled with white people, and the conductor ordered Smalls to give up his seat and move outside.

Smalls argued that he had just as much right to a seat as anyone. And his friend explained that Captain Smalls was a war hero serving the United

States of America. The conductor insisted they move. Smalls and his friend got off and walked rather than suffer the indignity of riding on the platform.

Newspapers in Philadelphia, New York, and other cities reported the story of the Negro hero who had been denied a seat on a city streetcar. The incident inspired Philadelphia blacks to protest against the streetcar companies. Three years later, a new Pennsylvania law forbade discrimination on streetcars and all other public transportation.

In late 1864, Captain Smalls and the *Planter* steamed out of Philadelphia's harbor. He was in a hurry to return home. Newspapers had been reporting the daily progress of Union General William T. Sherman's huge army, which was burning a swath across Georgia and would soon attack South Carolina.

6

War's End

When he docked the *Planter* at Beaufort, Captain Smalls found the town in a state of excitement. General Sherman and his army of sixty thousand men, on their famous "march to the sea," had burned Atlanta. Next they easily captured Savannah, and the general presented the old coastal city to President Lincoln as a "Christmas present." Now Sherman was preparing to invade South Carolina.

Smalls immediately went to work. "Some twenty steamers," one Sea Island resident wrote, "arrive daily at Beaufort direct from Savannah bringing the troops and wagons, artillery and animals."

The Confederate army in Charleston, badly outnumbered by Sherman's invaders, abandoned the cradle of the rebellion. As they retreated by land, boats full of federal troops steamed unchallenged past the deserted rubble of Fort Sumter into Charleston harbor.

Among the Union soldiers who occupied Charleston were several all-black companies. They proudly marched into the city singing "John

Black troops marching into the ruins of Charleston

Brown's Body," a song that was popular among black soldiers.

John Brown died that the slave might be free,
John Brown died that the slave might be free,
John Brown died that the slave might be free,
But his soul goes marching on!
Glory, Glory Hallelujah.

Most white people had fled, but the city's blacks, who had been held in slavery until that day, lined the streets cheering the liberating soldiers. Many of them rushed to join the Union army. In a single day, over three hundred freedmen took the military oath, swearing allegiance to the United States of America.

The invading troops found large sections of Charleston in ruins. The Confederates had pried cobblestones from the streets to build fortifications. A huge fire had burned several blocks in the center of town. Continual bombardment by Union cannons during the war's last year had reduced

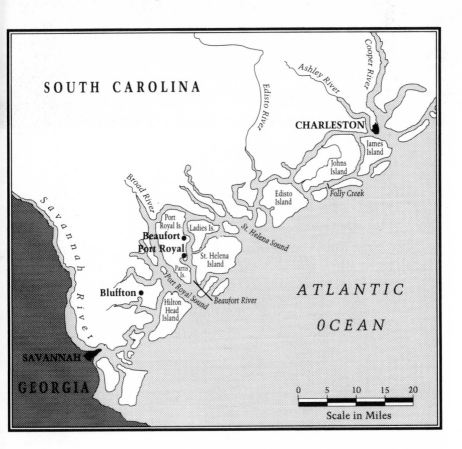

On the walls of Fort Sumter, Union soldiers watch the ships in Charleston harbor during the April 14 celebration.

houses and stores to fire-blackened brick walls and heaps of stones and charred timber.

The destruction could have been much worse, but Sherman's army spared Charleston. It bypassed the coastal city and attacked Columbia, the state capital. South Carolina, unlike Georgia, offered little resistance to the invaders. Sherman's troops easily conquered the state and marched on to North Carolina.

A few weeks later, the war ended. General Robert E. Lee, the commander of the Confederate army, surrendered to General Ulysses S. Grant, the commander of the Union army, on April 9 at Appomattox Courthouse, Virginia.

Beaufort's residents greeted the news of victory and peace with relief and happiness. They quickly organized a festive celebration in Charleston on April 14, exactly four years after federal troops had surrendered Fort Sumter.

The day of the celebration, Charleston's churches rang their bells, bands played lively patriotic tunes, and forts fired their cannons. Gunboats, steamers, blockade runners, and monitors filled the harbor. From their riggings, thousands of colorful flags fluttered and snapped in the wind. Around mid-morning, ships teeming with passengers began making their way through the busy harbor. They were going to Fort Sumter for the main ceremony.

On the docks hundreds of people cheered, sang, and waved to passing ships. The *Planter*, an observer noted, was "crowded to almost suffocation upon her three decks . . . all huddled together like sheep in a pen, hanging over the gunwales, mounted on the posts, doubled up in furtive corners, peering through the gangways, darkening the wheelhouse, upon the top of which stood Robert Small, a prince among them, self-possessed, prompt and proud, giving his orders to the helmsman in ringing tones of command."

A hearty cheer welcomed the *Planter* when it arrived at Sumter. The passengers disembarked at a small dock. They walked into the fort between two rows of soldiers. One row was black and the other row was white. These men stood proudly at attention with their rifles on their shoulders, bayonets gleaming in the sun.

In Sumter, the civilians marveled at the destruction. Four years earlier, the fort had been five stories tall; now it was barely one story. Constant bombardment had destroyed its high, thick walls. Cannonballs, broken bricks, and splintered timbers covered the ground.

The ceremony began with Major Robert Anderson raising a tattered and smoke-stained American flag. This was the same flag that Major Anderson, as Union commander of the fort, had been forced to lower four years earlier after surrendering Sumter to the Confederates. When the Stars and Stripes reached the top of the pole, the crowd of onlookers gave a long, loud cheer. The soldiers standing at attention along the parapet raised their rifles and fired a one-hundred-gun salute.

"Came the thunder of mighty cannon in national salute" as other forts and warships joined in, one eyewitness reported, "until the earth shook and trembled, and the air grew dark with the gathering clouds of smoke which rolled their dun and murky volume over the harbor, shutting out from sight at length the city."

The smoky, thundering salute lasted a full half hour. Then came several long speeches, one by the famous New York minister and abolitionist Henry Ward Beecher. Afterward, the crowd streamed back onto the ships. The *Planter* led the procession of vessels back to the city.

The festivities continued late into the night. At dusk, the lighting of hundreds of lanterns hanging from every ship in the harbor created a dazzling blaze of light. Later, a brilliant display of Roman candles filled the night sky. The evening's big event, similar to the one four years earlier when the Confederates celebrated the fall of Sumter, was a fancy dress ball. It was held in a grand mansion that had been the home of a Confederate general.

That night Captain Smalls visited the *Oceanus*, a ship that had brought people from New York for the Charleston celebration. He entertained its passengers by telling them how he escaped from slavery. The northern visitors were impressed by the story and by the man. "The famous Negro captain of the steamboat *Planter*," observed one of the passengers, "is able to give bread to half the bank presidents and brokers" in Charleston. He is "regarded by all the other Negroes as immensely rich," and one of the smartest men in South Carolina.

On the evening of April 14, while people in Charleston were celebrating the end of the war, President Abraham Lincoln was shot in the back of the head as he watched a play at Ford's Theater in downtown Washington. He died the next day. The assassin was John Wilkes Booth, a Southerner angry about losing the war. It took two days for news of the president's death to reach Charleston.

Only three years earlier, Captain Smalls had been an unknown slave called Robert. Now he was a hero praised by whites and blacks alike. As with many men and women who had been born into bondage, freedom gave Robert Smalls a chance to display the bravery and intelligence long suppressed by slavery.

7

King of Beaufort

The bloodiest war in American history was over. And Robert Smalls had become a prosperous man and an important leader. He was so influential some people called him King of Beaufort. This title was appropriate for two reasons.

Captain Smalls had been a well-paid boat pilot, so he had more money than most people in Beaufort. Many of the town's residents were freedmen who were just beginning to acquire land and other possessions. The plantations of once wealthy white people had been seized by federal officials and sold at public auction.

Smalls bought a plantation, several buildings, and, for only $600, the old McKee house where he had lived as a young slave. Before the war, the McKee family had moved to a plantation near Charleston. The family's former residence in Beaufort, a two-story house with chandeliers hanging in the parlor and the dining room, became the new home for Captain Smalls; his wife, Hannah;

and their children. The family employed a maid to care for the house and a coachman to drive their carriage.

People called the ex-slave King of Beaufort mainly because of his political power. Smalls's career in politics had begun during the war. The popular hero was one of four blacks from the Sea Islands who had been chosen to attend the 1864 Republican National Convention in Baltimore, Maryland, where Abraham Lincoln had been overwhelmingly nominated for a second term as president. The four men were the first African-Americans chosen to attend a national political convention as delegates. For the twenty-five-year-old boat pilot, it was the start of a long, often difficult career.

After the war, there was a twelve-year period known as Reconstruction. Federal soldiers policed the South to prevent violence between freedmen and white people. In 1865, Congress had created a special organization called the Freedmen's Bureau to help ex-slaves acquire education, jobs, and homes.

Now that they were free, African-Americans insisted on being treated as equal citizens. Many white people did not like this new relationship. A bitter man in Beaufort declared: "The infernal sassy niggers had better look out or they'll get their throats cut yet . . . Let a nigger come into my office without taking off his hat and he'll get a club. . . . "

48

White Southerners believed ex-slaves should remain maids and plantation laborers. They even passed laws, known as the Black Code, calling freedmen servants and whites masters. Should black men be allowed to vote? Should African-Americans have the same rights as whites? These and other important questions started a long struggle between the races.

This struggle was often violent. Former bondsmen were beaten for attending school. Some were murdered for refusing to work for their old masters. Others were killed because they voted or ran for political office. In 1868, the first year blacks were permitted to vote and to hold public office, a member of the state constitutional convention and three state legislators were murdered. "Political times are simply frightful," one observer noted. "Men are shot at, hounded down, trapped, and . . . intimidated in every possible way."

Captain Smalls plunged into politics. He helped organize South Carolina's first Republican party. Then, in early 1868, he was elected a delegate to the state constitutional convention. Over half of the 124 delegates to that convention were black. South Carolina, like every former Confederate state, rewrote its laws. "Neither slavery nor involuntary servitude," the new constitution declared, "shall be re-established within this state." It gave blacks, and even poor whites, rights they had never enjoyed. These rights included free public education for children, equal protection of the law, and the right to vote and to run for public office.

That same year, Smalls ran for state legislator in a special spring election. His campaign entertained voters with dramatic torchlight parades through the streets of Beaufort. These processions were led by Allen's Brass Band, an all-black marching band smartly dressed in navy blue uniforms.

In the Sea Islands, blacks vastly outnumbered whites and they were eager to vote. In Beaufort, there were ten blacks for one white person. On St. Helena Island, there were six thousand blacks and only seventy whites. In the 1868 election, throughout the state, nearly nine out of ten eligible blacks cast ballots. Although fifty thousand whites were registered to vote, only slightly more than half actually voted. Most blacks voted for Republican candidates, while most whites voted for Democratic candidates.

Soon after black men began voting, one visitor to Beaufort commented, "City Hall is controlled by the blacks, and the magistrates, the police, and the representatives to the Legislature are nearly all Africans."

No African-American in the short history of the United States had held elective office before the war. After the 1868 election, 82 of the 155 men in the South Carolina legislature were African-American. Many of them, like Captain Smalls, had been in the war. William H. W. Gray, a Charleston free black who had worked as a barber, had served as a sergeant in the Fifty-fourth Massachusetts. He had been wounded in the famous attack on Battery Wagner. Another legislator, Prince Rivers, had been a slave and a coachman in Beaufort. He had been a sergeant and the highest-ranking black in the First South Carolina Volunteers.

Stephen A. Swails, a boatman from Pennsylvania, had been a lieutenant in the Fifty-fourth Massachusetts. Although wounded, he distinguished himself for "coolness, bravery, and efficiency" in a bloody battle at Olustee, Florida, where the Union army suffered over eighteen hundred casualties.

Francis A. Cardoza was a free black from Charleston who had been educated at the University of Edinburgh in Scotland. During Reconstruction, he was a state legislator and then secretary of state.

For six years, Smalls served in the state legislature, first as a legislator and then as a state senator. In 1874, Sea Island voters elected him to the U.S. Congress. A Charleston newspaper commented on the Beaufort politician's popularity: "It is perfectly astonishing to witness the increasing influence of this Negro. He seems to possess the confidence of his race to a degree that no other Negro can hope to attain. The men, women and children seem to regard him with a feeling akin to worship."

This feeling was not shared by some white

The official photograph of Congressman Robert Smalls

people. The last federal peace-keeping troops left the South in 1877, ending Reconstruction. Then whites redoubled efforts to force blacks out of public life. One of their first targets was Congressman Smalls. They accused him of accepting a five-thousand-dollar bribe in return for his support of a legislative bill.

At his trial, a jury of seven black and five white men found Smalls guilty. He was sentenced to three years in prison. A deal between state and federal officials spared the congressman that long ordeal. The governor released him from jail after only three days.

No one knows if Congressman Smalls actually accepted the bribe. Most of his supporters believed the trial was politically motivated. The bribery conviction, according to a friend, had two purposes. "One is to prevent his taking his seat in the approaching congress, and the other to bring odium upon him and give his opponent in the contested seat a better chance."

Smalls was a target of white hatred in other ways too. During the fall campaign of 1878, as the congressman prepared to make a speech one morning in Gillisonville, a gang of white men on horseback galloped into town "giving the rebel yell and whooping like Indians." They rode through the streets hitting black men and women. Smalls's supporters wanted to attack the whites, but the congressman persuaded them to withdraw into a nearby store. There they were surrounded by a crowd of whites who fired gunshots into the building and threatened to set it afire. Word of the siege spread through the community, and dozens of blacks armed with guns, axes, and hoes came to the rescue. The white men galloped away, avoiding a major battle.

Smalls lost the 1878 election. He won reelection in 1880, lost the election in 1882, but won again in 1884. He lost again two years later, but the man who was elected died before taking office. Smalls won a special election in early 1887 and completed the deceased man's term in Congress.

During his many years in Washington, D.C., Congressman Smalls tried to secure money to repair the damage done to his Sea Island district in the war. This was a popular cause among the people Smalls represented, but it received little support from other congressmen. Smalls did support the building of a naval base on Parris Island not far from Beaufort. This base was providing many jobs for the people of the Sea Islands. In another session, he helped defeat a bill that would have required black people and white people to ride in separate cars on the nation's trains. After finishing his fifth congressional term in 1888, Smalls never held elective office again.

Only one other black man in that era, Joseph Hayne Rainey, was elected to Congress as many times as Robert Smalls. South Carolina elected its last black representative in 1894. After that, it was nearly a hundred years before the state sent another African-American to Congress.

8

The End of an Era

Even though he no longer held elective office, Smalls remained a hero in Beaufort. The former boat pilot often showed visitors the gold medal he had received in New York back in 1862. And he showed them a painting of the *Planter* that hung on the living room wall of his home on Prince Street.

When visitors asked what happened to the *Planter*, Smalls explained that the ship had met a heroic and tragic end. After the war, the federal government sold the battered boat at auction. The new owner used it to transport cotton and lumber up and down the Carolina coast. In March 1876, the steamer tried to rescue a ship caught in a violent storm near Cape Romain, north of Charleston. The *Planter* was lost at sea. Smalls, a congressman at the time, said it was like losing a member of his family.

Smalls enjoyed telling his children how he had "stolen" the *Planter*. Two of his children had been passengers on the ship during its daring early morning journey through Charleston harbor. One child, Robert, Jr., died of illness soon after Smalls and his family had settled in Beaufort. The second child, Elizabeth, had been four years old when she escaped from slavery with her parents. She attended school in Massachusetts and returned to Beaufort to become the town's postmistress and then secretary of Penn School, founded by missionaries for black children.

Smalls's other daughter, Sarah, was born during the Civil War. She too went to school in Massachusetts, to the Boston Conservatory of Music, and returned home to become an instructor at South Carolina Teachers College.

Hannah Smalls, Robert's wife since the days when both were teenage slaves in Charleston, died in 1883. Seven years later, Smalls married a schoolteacher, Annie Elizabeth Wigg. In 1892, they had a son, William. At a time when few people, white or black, attended college, William graduated from the University of Pittsburgh. He became a teacher and then an official for the Urban League, the well-known civil rights organization.

William Smalls grew up in an era of strict segregation. After Reconstruction ended in 1877, the all-white Democratic party came to dominate South Carolina politics and began shoving black people out of public life. African-Americans in Beaufort greatly outnumbered whites, but fewer of them were being elected to the posts of sheriff or judge,

Annie Wigg Smalls,
Robert's second wife

or to any other political office. As white Democrats
increased their control over local and state government, they made new rules to keep blacks from
voting.

Arguments within the Republican party helped
the Democrats gain power. Republican leaders
spent as much time fighting among themselves as
they did fighting the Democrats. In the election of
1888, Smalls and his friends supported white
Democratic candidates. Smalls was angry because
he had lost his party's nomination for sheriff.

A new constitutional convention in 1895 illustrated the changing status of blacks. Unlike the
constitutional convention in 1868, which was
attended by more than sixty African-Americans,
only six blacks were among the 160 men who

attended South Carolina's 1895 convention. In a widely reported speech, Smalls spoke forcefully against rewriting the state's most important legal document. He knew the changes would harm African-Americans. This was one battle he lost. The convention adopted a new constitution that prevented black people from voting and effectively made them second-class citizens.

The changes in the constitution reflected a new relationship between the races. Laws—called Jim Crow laws—said that whites and blacks should be separated in public places such as restaurants and trains. There were few schools for black children. Many jobs, even those that did not require formal education, were denied African-Americans. In stores, clerks waited on black customers last after every white customer had been helped. And blacks always had to address whites as mister or miss, while whites addressed blacks by only their first names. Blacks who challenged Jim Crow laws and customs were often beaten or lynched. In many ways, this new system of race relations was just as cruel as slavery.

Smalls's prominence protected him from many of the indignities of segregation. In 1890, President Benjamin Harrison appointed his fellow Republican politician customs collector for the Port of Beaufort. This was one of the highest positions in the state held by a black man. Smalls kept the job for over twenty years, finally retiring in

This last known photograph of Robert Smalls was probably taken at his desk in the customs house at Beaufort.

1913. Two years later, at the age of seventy-five, he died.

The former slave, Civil War hero, and leader was given the largest funeral Beaufort had ever seen. Robert Smalls was buried beside the African Methodist Episcopal Church on Craven Street. Today, visitors pause by his grave to read these words from his famous speech at the 1895 constitutional convention. "My race needs no special defenses. For the past history of them in this country proves them to be the equal of any people anywhere. All they need is an equal chance in the battle of life."

Glossary

abolitionist   a person who wanted to abolish slavery. Abolitionism, as a reform movement, began in the United States about 1830.

battery   an artillery unit or cannon usually protected by an earthen wall

blockade   the closing by military force of a port, city, or coast to prevent traffic and communication by hostile forces

constitutional convention   a meeting of elected representatives in order to write, or rewrite, their government's basic laws

Emancipation Proclamation   one of the most important acts of the Civil War. It became law on January 1, 1863, and declared slaves in the rebelling states to be free. Although Confederates forcibly held most slaves, the proclamation encouraged thousands to flee their plantations, which deprived the South of valuable labor. It also permitted ex-slaves to join the Union army and help defeat the Confederates.

free blacks   Several thousand free blacks lived in the South before the Civil War. Some had been freed by their owners. Others had managed to purchase their own freedom or were descendants of slaves granted freedom because they had fought in the Revolutionary War.

Gullah   a language combining English and African words spoken by blacks living in the Sea Islands of South Carolina and Georgia

ironclad   a nineteenth-century warship with metal-plated sides

Jim Crow   the name, taken from a fictional character in a minstrel show, given to the system of southern laws and customs discriminating against black people

monitor   a type of nineteenth-century ironclad warship with a low, flat deck and one or two gun turrets. The first Union vessel with this design was named the *Monitor.*

parapet   the wall of a fort

plantation   large farm where crops such as cotton, tobacco, or sugar are cultivated by resident laborers

racism   the opinion that people of one race are superior to people of other races

Reconstruction   the period from 1865 to 1877 when the federal government controlled the eleven former states of the Confederacy and forced them to accept laws providing fair and equal treatment for African-Americans in order to be readmitted to the Union

Sea Islands approximately one hundred sub-tropical islands along the coasts of South Carolina and Georgia

secede to officially withdraw from an association or government

segregation the separation of races in schools, jobs, housing, and other areas of daily life

Chronology

1839 Robert Smalls born in Beaufort, South Carolina, April 5.

1851 At age twelve, Robert is sent to Charleston.

1860 The *Planter* is launched in Charleston harbor.

Abraham Lincoln elected president of the United States in November.

1860- South Carolina votes to secede December 20, 1860. In January 1861, Mississippi, Florida, Alabama, Georgia, and Louisiana follow. By June, five other states, Texas, Virginia, Arkansas, Tennessee, and North Carolina secede to complete the Confederate States of America.

1861 Civil War begins April 12 when South Carolina troops fire on Fort Sumter.

Union navy captures Port Royal Sound November 7.

1862 The *Planter*, piloted by Robert Smalls, escapes Charleston May 13.

First South Carolina Volunteers is organized in November.

1863 The Emancipation Proclamation becomes law on January 1.

Monitors and ironclads attack Charleston April 7.

At dusk on July 18, the Fifty-fourth Massachusetts Infantry attacks Battery Wagner.

Smalls made captain of the *Planter* in August.

1864 Captain Smalls sails the *Planter* to Philadelphia on May 10.

In early December, Smalls's argument on a Philadelphia streetcar calls attention to discrimination against blacks.

The ship and its captain return to Beaufort on December 24.

1865 General William T. Sherman attacks South Carolina on January 16.

Civil War ends April 9, when Robert E. Lee, commander of the Confederate army, surrenders to General Ulysses S. Grant, commander of the Union army, at Appomattox Courthouse, Virginia.

Abraham Lincoln shot by assassin on April 14. He dies the next day.

The Freedmen's Bureau established in March. It helps provide former slaves with food, transportation, schools, assistance in getting jobs, and fair wages. The bureau also settles freedmen on abandoned or confiscated lands.

1868 South Carolina adopts a new constitution in March.

Smalls elected to South Carolina legislature in April.

1874 Smalls wins his first term in the U.S. Congress.

1876 The *Planter* lost in a March storm near Cape Romain, South Carolina.

Smalls reelected to Congress.

1877 Reconstruction ends when Rutherford B. Hayes becomes president.

Congressman Smalls, although convicted for bribery, is pardoned by the governor of South Carolina.

1878 Smalls loses his seat in Congress in the November election.

1880 Smalls wins his third congressional term.

1882 Congressman Smalls loses the November election.

1883 Hannah Smalls dies July 28.

1884 Smalls reelected to Congress.

1887 In a special election, Smalls wins his fifth congressional term.

1888 Smalls finishes his last term in Congress.

1890 President Benjamin Harrison in January appoints Smalls customs collector for the Port of Beaufort.

Annie Elizabeth Wigg marries Smalls April 9.

1895 South Carolina adopts new state constitution December 4.

1913 Smalls retires as customs collector.

1915 Robert Smalls dies February 22.

Index

Page numbers in *italics* refer to photographs.

abolitionists, 2
Africa, 14
African-Americans:
  in Charleston, 15–16, 40–41
  at 1864 Republican National Convention, 48
  at 1868 Constitutional Convention, 49–50, 57
  at 1895 Constitutional Convention, 57–58
  in Philadelphia, 36–38
  in Reconstruction, 48–52
  in South Carolina legislature, 50–51
  in U.S. Congress, 51–54
  as viewed by white people, 25–26, 33, 48–49
  voting rights of, 49, 50, 57–58
  see also slaves, slavery
African-American soldiers:
  discrimination against, 23–25
  pay of, 24, 26
  recruitment of, 21–25, *24*, 37
  see also Fifty-fourth Massachusetts Infantry; First South Carolina Volunteers

Allen's Brass Band, 50
"America," 28
Anderson, Robert, 44
Appomattox Courthouse, Virginia, 43
Ashley River, *5*, 15, *41*
Atlanta, Georgia, 39
Atlantic Ocean, *5*, *41*

Baltimore, Maryland, 48
Battery Wagner, *5*, 32–33, 51
Beaufort, South Carolina, 12, 13, *13*, 25, 39, *41*, 56, 58, 59
  African-American suffrage in, 50
  Smalls as King of, 47–54, 55
  Union capture of, 3, 7, 22
Beaufort River, 27, *41*
Beecher, Henry Ward, 45
Black Code, 49
Bluffton, Georgia, 25
Booth, John Wilkes, 46
Broad River, *41*

Cape Romain, South Carolina, 55
Cardoza, Francis A., 51
Catskill, 29

Charleston, South Carolina, 1, 2–3, *5*, 8, 15–19, *41*
African-Americans in, 15–16, 40–41
April 14th celebration in, 42–46, *42*
control of slaves in, 17
defense of, 7, 19, 26, 29–35, 39
destruction of, *40*, 41–42, 44
naval blockade of, 3, 10, 33
population of, 15
Stars and Stripes raised in, 44
Union assaults on, 19, 29–33, *31*, 39–40
Citadel, The, *5*
Civil War, U.S.:
Lee's surrender in, 42–43
start of, 2–3, 19
see also Confederate States of America; Union
Columbia, South Carolina, 42
Confederate States of America (CSA):
Charleston defended by, 7, 19, 29–35, 39–40
Fort Sumter won by, 2–3, *5*, 43, 44, 45
Planter used by, 7, 8, *9*, 19
retreat from Charleston by, 39
secession of, 2
surrender of, 42-43
Congress, U.S., 48, 51, 54

Constitutional Conventions, South Carolina:
of 1868, 49–50, 57
of 1895, 57–58
contrabands, 22
Cooper River, *5*, 15, *41*
Coosawhatchie River, 22

Daniel Island, *5*
Democratic party, 50, 56–57
Drum Island, *5*
DuPont, Samuel, 10–11, 24, 29–30, 31, 32

Edisto Island, *13*, *41*
Edisto River, *41*
elections:
Congressional, 51, 53–54, 57
state and local, 50–51, 57
Emancipation Day, 27–28, *27*
Emancipation Proclamation (1863), 26–27, 28

Fifty-fourth Massachusetts Infantry, 32–33, 51
First South Carolina Volunteers, 22, 25, 27, 51
Folly Creek, 33, *41*
Ford's Theater, 45
Freedmen's Bureau, 48
French, Mansfield, 21

Georgia, 22, 25, 38, *41*, 42
Gillisonville, 53

Grant, Ulysses S., 42–43
Gray, William H. W., 50–51
Gullah, 14

Harper's Weekly, 1, *35*
Harrison, Benjamin, 58
Hilton Head Island, *41*

ironclads, 29–32

Jacksonville, Florida, 25
James Island, *5*, 33, *41*
Jim Crow laws, 58
"John Brown's Body," 39–40
Johns Island, *41*
Johnson, Fort, *5*

Keokuk, 29–30, 32

Ladies Island, 13, *41*
Lee, Robert E., 42–43
Lincoln, Abraham, 2, 39, 48
    assassination of, 45–46
    Emancipation
       Proclamation
       signed by, 26
    and recruitment of
       African-Americans, 21
Lydia (mother), 12–13

McKee, Henry, 14–15, 16
McKee family, 12–13, 22, 47
monitors, 29–32, 43
Montauk, 29
Morris Island, *5*, 30, 33
Moultrie, Fort, *5*, 30, *31*, 32
Mt. Pleasant, *5*

Nahant, 29, 32
Nantucket, 29
New Ironsides, 29-31
New York, New York, 20–21,
    55

Oceanus, 45
Olustee, Florida, battle of, 51
Onward, 4–5

Parris Island, *41*, 54
Passaic, 29
Patapsco, 29
Penn, Camp, 37
Penn School, 56
Philadelphia, Pennsylvania,
    36–38
Pittsburgh, University of, 56
Planter, 1, 4–11, *6*, 19, 20,
    34, *35*, 55–56
    in April 14th celebration,
       43, 45
    as CSA transport, 7, 8, *9*,
       19
    repairs to, 36, 38
    Smalls made captain of,
       34–35
    Smalls's rescue of, 33–35
    Smalls's stories about, 55–
       56
    Union use of, *9*, 33–35
Planters Hotel, 16
Port Royal Sound, South
    Carolina, 3, *13*, *41*

Rainey, Joseph Hayne, 54
Reconstruction, 48–52, 56

Republican National
    Convention (1864), 48
Republican party, 48, 49,
    50, 57
Richmond, Virginia, 10
Ripley, Roswell, 19
Ripley, Fort, *5*
Rivers, Prince, 28, 5l

St. Helena Island, *41*, 50
St. Helena Sound, *41*
St. Michael's Episcopal
    Church, 17
Savannah, Georgia, 3, 39, *41*
Savannah River, 22, *41*
Saxton, Rufus, 21
Sea Islands, 3, 13–14, 19,
    21, 22, 27–28, *27*, 36,
    41, 48, 50, 51, 54
Secessionville, South
    Carolina, 33
Seymour, Truman, 24–25
Shaw, Robert Gould, 33
Sherman, William T., 38–39,
    42
Shiloh Church, 20–21
slaves, slavery:
    as cause of Civil War, 2–3
    city vs. plantation, 15
    education of, 1, 17
    family life of, 12–13
    hiring out of, 16–17
    names of, 12, 17
    punishment of, 14, 17
    as viewed by white people,
        11, 16
Smalls, Annie Elizabeth
    Wigg (second wife), 56,
    57

Smalls, Elizabeth (daughter),
    56
Smalls, Hannah (first wife),
    8, 17-18, *18*, 47, 56
Smalls, Robert, *6*, *18*, *34*, *35*,
    52, *59*
    birth of, 12
    bravery of, 11, 21, 25, 34,
        46
    at 1868 Constitutional
        Convention, 49
    at 1895 Constitutional
        Convention, 57–58, 59
    convicted of bribery, 52
    as customs collector, 58–
        59
    death and funeral of, 59
    discrimination faced by,
        24–25, 52–53
    elected to South Carolina
        state legislature, 50–51
    elected to U.S. Congress,
        51, 53
    escape from slavery by,
        1, 4–11, 19, 45, 55–56
    fame of, 1, 2, 20, 46, 55
    gold medal presented to,
        20, 55
    hiring out of, 16–17, 18–
        19
    as house servant, 14–15
    income of, 26, 45, 47
    intelligence of, 1, 11, 45,
        46
    marriages of, *see* Smalls,
        Hannah; Smalls, Annie
        Elizabeth Wigg
    in naval assault on
        Charleston, 29–32

72

piloting expertise of, 7, 8, 26, 34
plantation purchased by, 47
political career of, 47–54, 57–58
recruitment of African-Americans by, 21–25
streetcar incident and, 36–38
Smalls, Robert, Jr. (son), 56
Smalls, Sarah (daughter), 56
Smalls, William (son), 56
Smith Plantation, 27
South Carolina, 13, 19, 22, 41, 49–58
    African-American legislators in, 49–51, 54, 56–58
    African-American suffrage in, 50, 58
    1868 Constitutional Convention in, 49–50
    1895 Constitutional Convention in, 57–58
    Jim Crow laws in, 58
    Union invasion of, 7, 38–40, 42
    South Carolina Teachers College, 56
Stanton, Edwin M., 21

Sullivan Island, 5, 30
Sumter, Fort, 3, 5, 8–10, 30, 31, 32–33, 39, 42, 44, 45, 51
Swails, Stephen A., 51

Union (United States):
    African-American soldiers in, see African-American soldiers
    Beaufort captured by, 3, 7, 22
    Charleston invaded by, 19, 39–40
    Fort Sumter surrendered by, 2–3, 43, 44, 45
    naval assault on Charleston by, 29–32, 31
    naval blockade by, 1, 3–4, 10, 13
    Planter used by, 9, 33–35
    Port Royal Sound captured by, 3, 13
    reaction to Smalls's escape in, 10–11
    South Carolina invaded by, 7, 38–40, 42
Urban League, 56

Washington, D.C., 21, 32, 45, 54
Weehawken, 29, 30

About the Author

MICHAEL L. COOPER was born in the coal mining town of Gatliff, Kentucky. A graduate of the University of Kentucky, he is completing a Ph.D. in American history at the City University of New York. A professional writer for fifteen years, Mr. Cooper has done articles for various publications, including *Outdoor Life, Travel & Leisure,* and the *Washington Post.* He is the author of three other books for children, most recently *Playing America's Game: The Story of Negro League Baseball.* He lives in New York City.

About the Illustrations

The camera was not invented until the 1840s, and photography was still a crude art at the time of the Civil War. Newspapers and magazines illustrated stories with drawings done by artists, who would quickly sketch their subjects and send material by courier or mail. Most of the drawings that appear in this book were originally used during the Civil War to accompany news accounts. Photography became popular during the war, and photographers eventually replaced the quick sketch artists.

DATE			